Contents

What you need to know about the National Tests

Preparing and practising for the Maths Test

Instructions	1
Test A (Levels 4–6)	2
Test B (Levels 4–6)	17
Test C (Levels 5–7)	28
Test D (Levels 5–7)	39
Mental Test	51
Answers	52
Mental Test Questions	71
Formulae	72
Determining your level	73
Marking Grid	74

What you need to know about the National Tests

KEY STAGE 3 NATIONAL TESTS: HOW THEY WORK

Students between the ages of 11 and 14 (Years 7–9) cover Key Stage 3 of the National Curriculum. In May of their final year of Key Stage 3 (Year 9), all students take written National Tests (commonly known as SATs) in English, Mathematics and Science. The tests are carried out in school, under the supervision of teachers, but are marked by examiners outside the school.

The tests help to show what you have learned in these key subjects. They also help parents and teachers to know whether students are reaching the standards set out in the National Curriculum. The results may be used by your teacher to help place you in the appropriate teaching group for some of your GCSE courses.

Each student will probably spend around seven hours in total sitting the tests during one week in May. Most students will do two test papers in each of English, Mathematics and Science.

The school sends the papers away to external examiners for marking. The school will then report the results of the tests to you and your parents by the end of July, along with the results of assessments made by teachers in the classroom, based on your work throughout Key Stage 3. You will also receive a summary of the results for all students at the school, and for students nationally. This will help you to compare your performance with that of other students of the same age. The report from your school will explain to you what the results show about your progress, strengths, particular achievements and targets for development. It may also explain how to follow up the results with your teachers.

UNDERSTANDING YOUR LEVEL OF ACHIEVEMENT

The National Curriculum divides standards for performance in each subject into a number of levels, from one to eight. On average, students are expected to advance one level for every two years they are at school. By Year 9 (the end of Key Stage 3), you should be at Level 5 or 6. The table on page iii shows how you are expected to progress through the levels at ages 7, 11 and 14 (the end of Key Stages 1, 2 and 3).

There are different National Test papers for different ability levels. This is to ensure that you can show positive achievement on the test, and not be discouraged by trying to answer questions which are too easy or too difficult. For Maths, the tests are grouped into four ranges of levels, called 'tiers'. The four tiers cover Levels 3–5, Levels 4–6, Levels 5–7 and Levels 6–8. Your teachers will decide which tier you should be entered for. Each tier has two test papers, one in which you may not use a calculator and one in which you may. Each paper will be one hour long. You may also take a mental arithmetic test as part of a national pilot in 1997, although the results of this pilot test will not affect your overall level in Maths. Extension papers with questions above Level 8 are also available for exceptionally able students.

What you need to know about the National Tests

How you should progress

This book concentrates on Levels 4–7, providing two test papers for Levels 4–6 and two papers for Levels 5–7. This means that you will find plenty of questions to practise, regardless of which tier you are entered for. The bar chart below shows you what percentage of students nationally reached each of the levels in the 1996 tests for Maths.

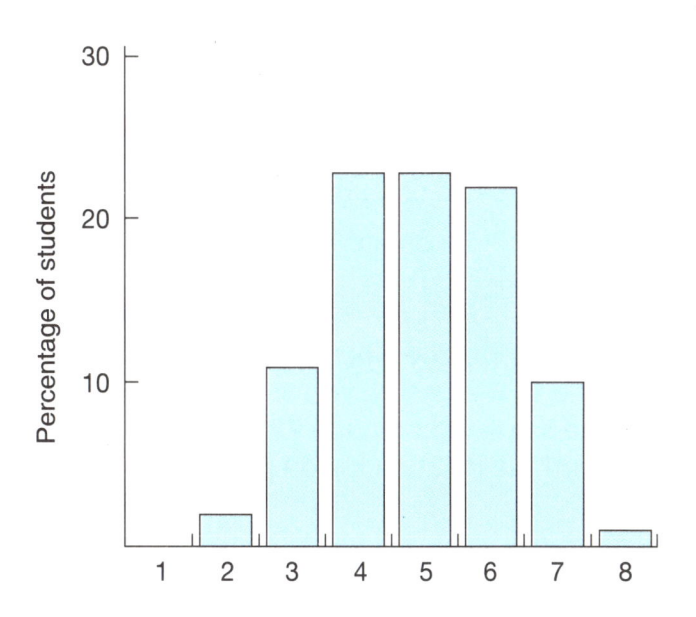

Levels achieved in Mathematics, 1996

Preparing and practising for the Maths Test

MATHS AT KEY STAGE 3
The questions in this book will test you on the Key Stage 3 curriculum for Mathematics. For assessment purposes, the National Curriculum divides Mathematics into four sections, called Attainment Targets (ATs). The first AT, Using and Applying Mathematics, is assessed only by the teacher in the classroom, not in the written tests. The other three ATs are:
- AT2: Number and Algebra
- AT3: Shape, Space and Measures
- AT4: Handling Data

The National Curriculum describes levels of performance for each of the four Mathematics ATs. These AT levels are taken together to give an overall level for Mathematics. The test papers have questions covering each of ATs 2–4.

USING THIS BOOK TO HELP YOU PREPARE
This book contains four basic features:

Questions:	one non-calculator and one calculator test paper for both Levels 4–6 and Levels 5–7, and one (optional) mental arithmetic test
Answers:	showing acceptable responses and marks
Examiner's Tips:	giving advice on how to avoid common mistakes and improve your score
Level Charts:	showing you how to interpret your marks to arrive at a level for each test and overall

SETTING THE TESTS AT HOME
Try taking Tests A and B (on different days) first. Mark each test to see how you have done. If your results indicate that you are working at Level 4 or higher, then you should try Tests C and D, which are more challenging, sometime later. Work through the answers and advice given to see where you might have done better on Tests A and B. When you've had a chance to improve your understanding, take Tests C and D on different days.

You should carry out the tests in a place where you are comfortable. You will need the equipment listed on page vi. Make sure you are familiar with the formulae you need to use. These formulae are listed on page 72, which you should detach and refer to during the tests. Read the instructions on page 1 carefully before you begin.

Preparing and practising for the Maths Test

Note the starting time in the box at the top of each test. Time yourself during the test, using a clock, a watch, or the help of a parent or friend. During the test, if you do not understand a word, you can ask a parent or other adult to explain what the word means, providing it is not a mathematical word. For example, you could ask someone to explain what is meant by the word 'surrounding', but not 'quadrilateral' or 'decimal'.

After 60 minutes, stop writing. If you have not finished, but wish to continue working on the test, draw a line to show how much has been completed within the test time. Then continue for as long as you wish.

MARKING THE QUESTIONS

When you have completed a test, turn to the Answers section at the back of the book. Work through the answers, using the advice in the Examiner's Tips to correct mistakes and explain problems. If you required extra time to complete a test, go through all the answers, but do not include the marks for the 'extra' questions in the total scores.

Using the recommended answers, award yourself the appropriate mark or marks for each question. In the margin of each test page, there are small boxes divided in half. The marks available for each question are at the bottom; write your score in the top half of the box.

Enter the total number of marks for each question on the Marking Grid on page 74. Then add them up to find the total for the test. Look at the Level Charts on page 73 to determine your level for each test, as well as an overall level.

ABOUT THE MENTAL TEST

Working things out in your head is an important part of the National Curriculum. In 1997, a mental test will be introduced as a national pilot in which all schools may participate. The test will assess your mental recall and ability to deal with numerical problems. You may take one of these if your school participates in the pilot.

The results of this pilot will help to determine the exact nature of the test when it becomes compulsory in 1998. As with the national pilot, the mental test in this book is optional and will not contribute to your overall level in Mathematics. However, you may wish to use this test as extra practice, and to prepare yourself for the types of question you may encounter in the pilot test.

Preparing and practising for the Maths Test

EQUIPMENT YOU WILL NEED

The following equipment may be needed for answering these questions:

- a pen, pencil and rubber
- a ruler (30 cm plastic ruler is most suitable)
- a calculator, preferably a simple scientific calculator

- angle measurer or protractor

  The angle measurer is probably easier to use than the protractor, particularly for angles greater than 180°.

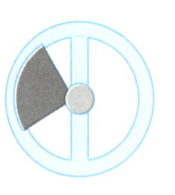

- tracing paper

  This is useful for rotational symmetry questions.

- a pair of compasses

  Use this for drawing circles.

- a mirror

  This is useful for symmetry questions.

FINALLY, AS THE TESTS DRAW NEAR

In the days before the tests, make sure you are as relaxed and confident as possible. You can help yourself by:

- ensuring you know what test papers you will be doing;

- working through practice questions, and learning which answers are right and why;

- checking that you have all the relevant equipment.

Above all, don't worry too much! Although the National Tests are important, your achievement throughout the school year is equally important. Do your best in these tests; that is all anyone can ask.

Instructions

Each test should take 60 minutes.

Try to answer all questions.

Read the questions carefully. If you think, after reading a question carefully, that you cannot answer it, leave the question and come back to it later.

The questions for you to answer are in blue boxes. For example,

> **How many 3 litre cans does Asif have to buy to cover an area of 254 square metres?**

Write your answers and working on the test papers in this book.
The ✏️ shows where you should answer the question. The lines or spaces should give you some indication of what is expected.

Look at the number of marks available for each part of a question. This is shown in the box in the margin, for example,

1

In Mathematics, marks are awarded for the method you use as well as the answer. It is important to show your working clearly so you can receive credit.

You must not use a calculator in Tests A or C, but a calculator may be used in Tests B and D.

Look carefully at the words you write, particularly mathematical words. Read your answers carefully to yourself and make sure you have clearly expressed what you mean.

GOOD LUCK!

Test A

TEST A — LEVELS 4–6

MARKS

WITHOUT CALCULATOR

Start ☐   Finish ☐

1 Look at these shapes.

> Which are congruent to **A**? Write **YES** or **NO** under each.

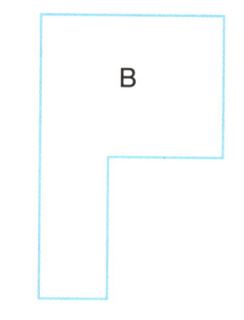

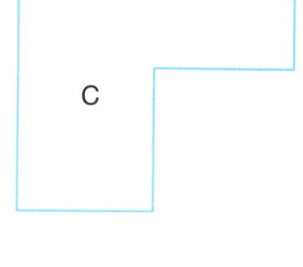

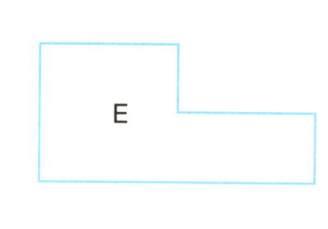

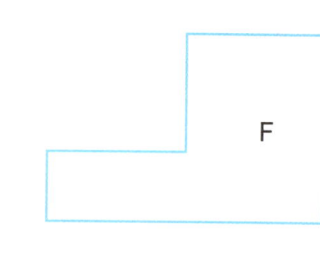

A   B   C

D   E   F

2 Mark does a survey of car colours in a car park.
He notes down each colour as he walks along the rows of cars.

W	W	B	R	R	G
G	G	W	R	B	B
R	R	G	W	R	R
B	B	B	W	R	R
B	G	R	R	W	W
B	B	G	R	R	W

W represents white, R represents red, B represents blue,
G represents green.

2 Q1

2

Test A

a Complete the frequency table.

Colour	Tally	Frequency
White		
Red		
Blue		
Green		

b Show the information as a bar chart.

TEST A
LEVELS 4–6

MARKS

c Sarah works at the local garage. She has recorded the colours of all the cars sold last year. The results are shown in the pie chart below.

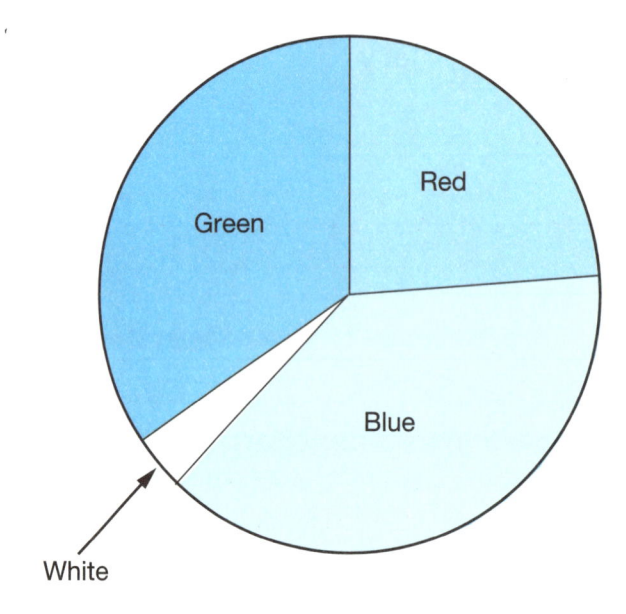

Which colour was the most popular? How can you tell this from the pie chart?

Colour: ....

....

....

2
Q2c

Test A

3 This is part of a table of 100 numbers:

Row 1	1	2	3	4	5	6	7	8	9	10
Row 2	11	12	13	14	15	16	17	18	19	20
Row 3	21	22	23	24	25	26	27	28	29	30

a **Which of these numbers are perfect squares?**

....

b The table is continued by adding five more rows.

What are the next two square numbers in the table and in which rows are they?

....

4 Two pints of milk cost 62p.

What is the cost of five pints of milk at the same price per pint?

....

....

Test A

5a Write down the next two terms in each of these number patterns.

(i) 1, 3, 5, 7, ...　　　　　　　　　........................　........................

(ii) 2, 4, 6, 8, ...　　　　　　　　　........................　........................

(iii) 3, 7, 11, 15, ...　　　　　　　........................　........................

b How is pattern (iii) connected to patterns (i) and (ii)?

....

6 Peter catches a train from Kings Cross to Edinburgh. The train leaves at 1030 and arrives in Edinburgh at 1556.

a How long did the journey take?

....

b Peter then catches another train to go to Dundee. This journey takes 1 hour and 14 minutes.

He leaves Edinburgh at 1650. What time does he arrive in Dundee?

....

6

Test A

7 Nadia draws some patterns on squared paper. She wants them to have either **reflection symmetry** or **rotational symmetry**.

Shade in the squares on each pattern to make them have:

a

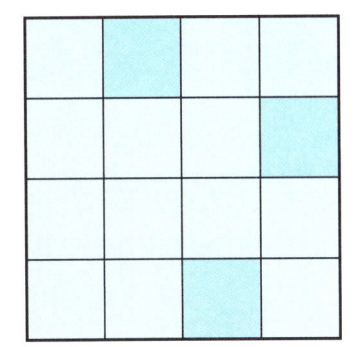

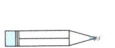

rotational symmetry of order 4 about the centre

b

reflection about the axis shown

c

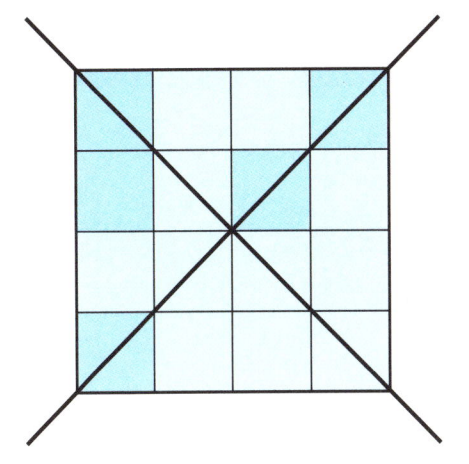

reflection about both axes

d

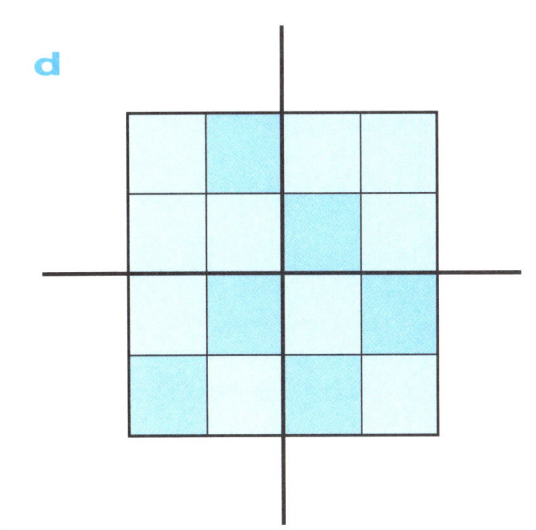

reflection about both axes

8   Diane is making a wedge to hold open a door.

Here is a sketch of the wedge.

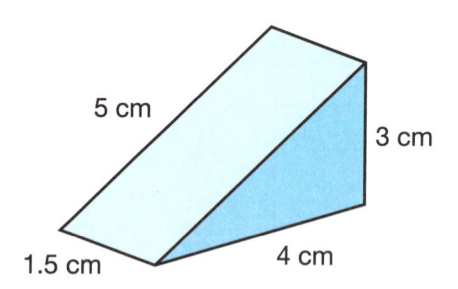

Complete this net for the wedge.

9 A bag contains 20 beads.

5 beads are grey, 9 beads are black and the rest are white.

Kim takes a bead at random from the bag.

a **What is the probability that it is black?**

....

b **What is the probability that it is not grey?**

....

10 Marcus needs to know approximately the weight of 28 tins of beans. He knows that one tin weighs 420 g. He estimates that 28 tins will weigh 12 000 g.

Show how he does this.

....

....

11 **Put the following numbers in size order, smallest first:**

1.457   154.7   1457.0   145.7   174.5   15.47

....

12 Part of a table of numbers is shown below. Look at the patterns.

1	2	4	8	A	
3	6	12	24		
9	18	36	72		B
27	54	108	216		
		C		D	

What numbers should be written in place of the letters?

A = ... B = ... C = ... D = ...

13 Sue's office door has a combination lock fitted. The door opens if you press four of the five numbered buttons in the right order. No button is pressed more than once.

1 2 3 4 5

Sue knows that the first two buttons to press are 3 followed by 4.

a **List all the possible combinations for the other two numbers.**

3rd digit	4th digit

10

Test A

TEST A
LEVELS 4-6

MARKS

b What is the probability that she finds the correct combination the first time?

....

1
Q13b

14 In the diagram **AB** = **BC** and **CD** is parallel to **AB**.

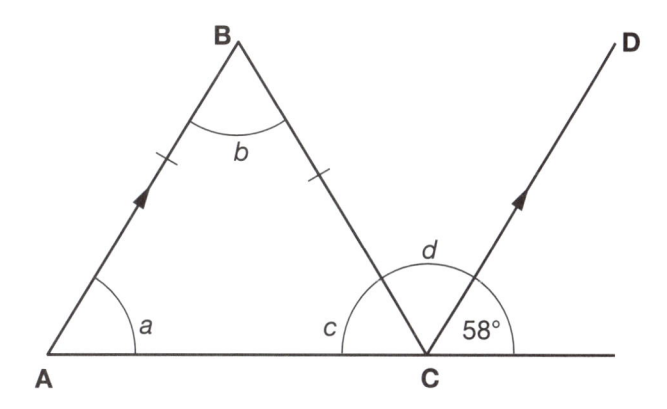

a Write down the size of angle *a*. Give a reason for your answer.

Angle *a* = ... degrees   Reason: ....

2
Q14a

b Write down the size of angle *d*. Give a reason for your answer.

Angle *d* = ... degrees   Reason: ....

2
Q14b

Test A

15 Tina is going shopping with her grandad. At the supermarket, she wants $\frac{1}{2}$ pound of cheese. They now sell cheese only in grams or kilograms.

a How much should she ask for?

....

b Tina buys some party invitations. They are 27p each and she buys 18.

Work out how much they will cost.

....

c Grandad buys 3 metres of ribbon. Tina knows that 1 inch is about $2\frac{1}{2}$ cm.

About how many inches are there in 3 metres?

....

d They want some tiles to fix to the bathroom wall.
The wall is 275 cm wide. Each tile is 15 cm wide.

How many whole tiles are needed in each row?

....

Test A

16 Here is a sketch plan of a field.

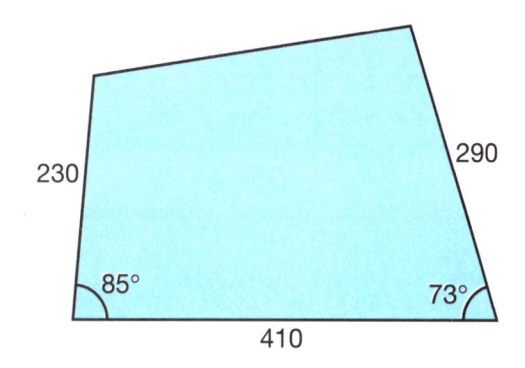

Peter and his friends have made the measurements shown. The distances are in metres.

a
Make a scale drawing of the field. Use a scale of 1 cm to 50 m.

The side representing 410 m has been drawn for you.

b
Measure the length of the fourth side.

How long is this on the field?

17 This is part of a table of 100 numbers:

1	2	3	4	5	6	7	8	9	10
11	12	13	14	15	16	17	18	19	20
21	22	23	24	25	26	27	28	29	30

10 of these numbers are prime numbers.

a **Complete the list of the prime numbers:**

2, 3, 5, 7, ..., ..., ..., 19, ..., ...

b Brian sets a puzzle for Pat. He chooses 3 numbers from the table and gives Pat the following clues:

'My first number is a prime number.'

'My second number is 3 times the first number.'

'My third number is 3 less than my second number.'

Test A

(i) **If the first number is *x*, write down in terms of *x* the second and third numbers.**

first number = x

second number = ...

third number = ...

(ii) When these three numbers are added together they have a total of 46.

Write down an equation in *x*.

....

(iii) **Use your equation to find the three numbers.**

....

....

18 The diagram shows one square card and one round card. Both cards have numbers on them, one on each side.

4　5

2　3

Lloyd is investigating the numbers he can make when he drops the two cards.

He drops both cards at the same time and looks at the two numbers that he can see.

Mark on the probability line the likelihood of the following results.

The first one is done for you.

A The two numbers add up to 10.　　**B** Both numbers are less than 6.

C The two numbers add up to 8.　　**D** One of the two numbers is even.

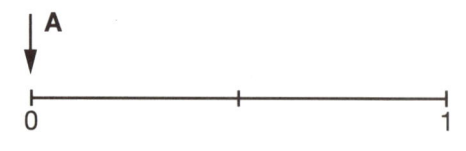

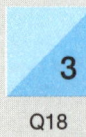

↓A
├─────────────┼─────────────┤
0　　　　　　　　　　　　　　　　　1

CALCULATOR CAN BE USED

Test B

Start ☐ Finish ☐

1 Kelly has been shopping.

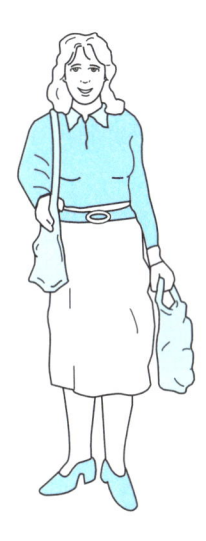

a She bought 6 kg of potatoes at 17p per kilogram.

How much did she pay for the potatoes?

£ ....

b Another day she bought these items:

Fruit	£0.63
Cheese	£1.74
Milk	£0.28
Bread	£0.65
Meat	£3.29

She paid with a £10 note.

How much change did she receive?

£ ....

c She also bought some clothes in a sale.

She paid £25 for a coat originally priced at £40.

> **What fraction of the original cost did she pay?**

d > **What percentage did she save?**

2 Sajid is a gardener. He uses a heated greenhouse in winter to grow his summer bedding plants.

a The temperature in the greenhouse has to be kept at a constant 15°C.

> **If the temperature outside is −7 °C what is the difference between this temperature and the temperature in the greenhouse?**

b Sajid will arrange the bedding plants round the edge of a circular flower bed in a park. The flower bed has a radius of 5 m. The plants have to be set 25 cm apart.

> **About how many plants will he need?**

3 In the UK, in 1991, there were 24.5 million vehicles. The forecast for 2010 is 36 million vehicles.

What is the percentage increase?

4 The typical diet of a sportsman is given on the table below:

Food type	%	Angle on a pie chart
Carbohydrate	60	216°
Fat	25	
Protein	15	

a **Add to the table by calculating the angle of the sector on a pie chart which represents fat.**

b **Draw the pie chart.**

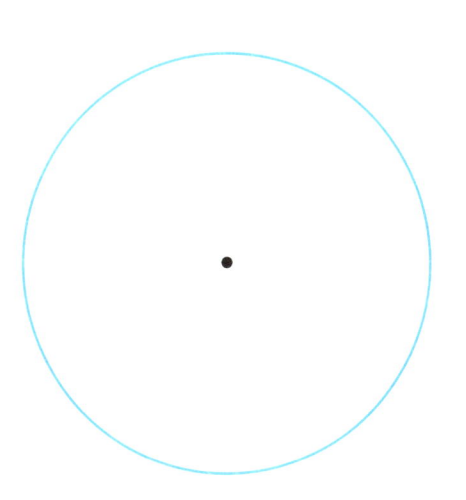

TEST B
LEVELS 4–6

MARKS

Test B

5 Dilanee is an electrician. She knows that electrical fuses are sold in the following ratings:

   3 amp   5 amp   13 amp

She calculates which is the correct fuse to be fitted to an appliance using the formula:

$$F = \frac{P}{240}$$ where F = fuse in amps and P = power rating in watts.

Which fuse should she fit to a hair dryer with a power rating of 1000 watts? Show your working.

2 — Q5

....

6 Brian is mixing cement to build a brick wall. He decides to mix cement in the ratio:

   3 parts cement   1 part lime   12 parts sand

a **What fraction of the mix will be sand?**

1 — Q6a

....

b **What percentage of the mix will be cement?**

1 — Q6b

....

c He uses 2 m³ of sand for the mix.

What volume of cement will he need?

1 — Q6c

.... m³

20

Test B

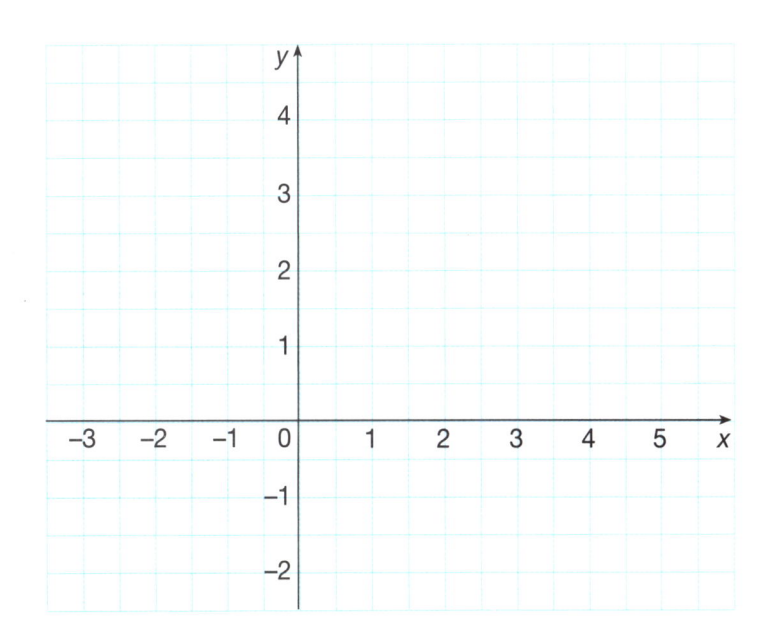

7 A Metro car is about 3.52 m long. The longest car in the world is 30.48 m long.

> **How many Metros would fit in this length?**

8a

(i) **Draw and label the graph of y = 2x −1.**

(ii) **Draw and label the graph of y = 3 − x.**

b **Write down the co-ordinates of the point where your two graphs meet.**

9 A washing machine costs £364 plus VAT.
VAT is charged at 17.5%.

a | How much is the VAT?

b | What is the total cost of the machine?

10 Amy and Tom are given this number puzzle:

'Find two numbers which add up to 20 and make 40 when multiplied together.'

Amy guesses 16 and 4.   Tom guesses 17.3 and 2.7.
16 + 4 = 20   17.3 + 2.7 = 20
16 × 4 = 64   17.3 × 2.7 = 46.71

Use the method of trial and improvement to find the two numbers as accurately as you can. Write down all your trials.

Test B

11 Daljit travels 25 000 miles each year on business. She gets paid 35p per mile travelling expenses.

a How much will she be paid?

b Her car will use 0.13 litres of petrol for each mile she drives.

How many litres of petrol will she need to buy?

c Petrol costs 56.9p per litre.

What is the cost of the petrol?

12 A camera is usually sold for £134. Snappers camera shop offer the camera with a reduction of 15%, while Camera Express are selling the same model with £20 off the usual price.

At which shop is the camera cheaper? Show your working.

13 Here are some instructions for a robot:

FORWARD 5
TURN RIGHT 90°
FORWARD 5
TURN RIGHT 90°
FORWARD 5
TURN RIGHT 90°
FORWARD 5

a Describe the shape that is formed when you follow these instructions.

b Write similar instructions to draw a rectangle measuring 3 units by 7 units.

14 Ruth's scores in Mathematics tests last year were 83, 86, 98, 87, and 96.

a Calculate Ruth's mean score.

b Calculate the range of Ruth's scores.

c Joan took the same tests. Her mean score was 89 and the range was 20. Ruth says that she did better than Joan.

Give one reason why you can agree with Ruth and one reason why you can disagree with her.

Agree ....

....

Disagree ....

....

15 Tower Bridge was opened in 1894.

        11 480 tonnes of iron and steel
        37 446 tonnes of concrete
        20 320 tonnes of cement
        27 696 tonnes of brick

were used in its construction.

What percentage of the total weight was brick?

....

....

16 This is a plan of Ajit's garden. The lengths are in metres.

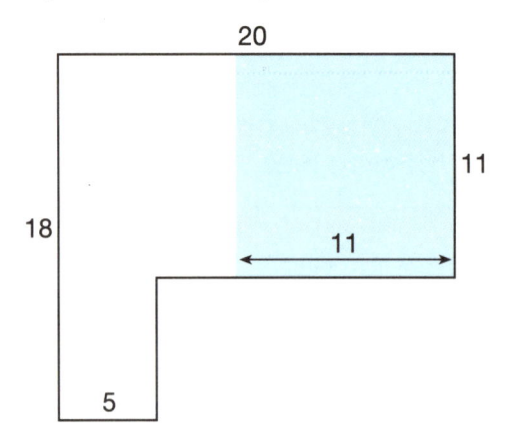

a Find the area of the whole garden.

b The shaded part is a lawn.

What percentage of the garden is lawn?

17 Jayne is paid £1800 for 45 days' work.

How much will she be paid for 12 days' work at the same rate?

18 A fifty pence coin weighs 13.5 g.

How heavy will £25 of fifty pence coins be in kilograms?

19 The cost of building a house is made up from wages, materials and overheads. In 1994, these costs were:

    materials   £21 000
    wages   £40 000
    overheads   £5000

a Find the total cost in 1994.

b In 1997, the cost will be more because:

    the cost of materials will have risen by 15%
    the cost of wages will have risen by 8%
    the overheads will have risen by 5%

(i) Calculate the total cost for 1997.

(ii) Calculate the percentage increase from 1994 to 1997.

TEST C
LEVELS 5–7

MARKS

WITHOUT CALCULATOR

Test C

Start ☐   Finish ☐

1 Asif is painting a warehouse. The special paint is sold in 3 litre cans. A 3 litre can of paint will cover an area of 17 square metres.

a How many 3 litre cans must he buy to cover 254 square metres?

....

....

....

b How much paint is not used?

....

....

....

c The area was measured as 254 m², correct to the nearest square metre.

What is the largest and smallest this area could be?

....

2 John has cut a grapefruit in half. Some of the pips have been cut in half as well. The cut pips are marked on the left-hand diagram.

Draw the pips on the right-hand picture.

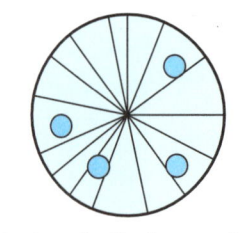

Bottom half of grapefruit 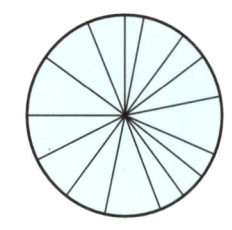   Top half of grapefruit

Q1a 2
Q1b 2
Q1c 2
Q2 2

28

3 The perimeter of this shape is *g* + *h*.

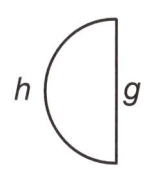

The perimeter of this shape is 4*g*.

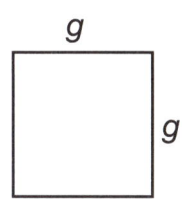

These shapes are combined to make new shapes.
Write down the perimeters of the new shapes.
Write your answers as simply as possible.

a

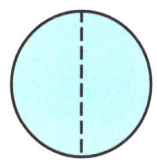

b

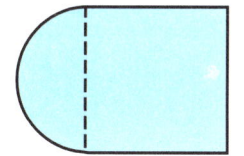

....

c

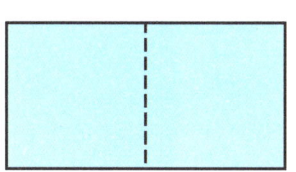

d

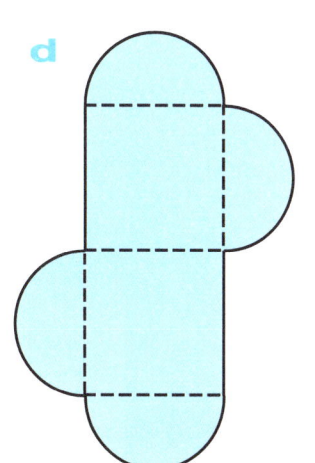

....

....

4 Abdul is mad about cars. He has collected this data.

Engine size (litres)	Cost now (£)
1.1	6500
1.4	8200
1.5	9000
1.2	7000
1.4	8300
1.5	9300
1.1	7300
1.6	10 000
1.8	12 000

a Draw a scatter diagram for this data.

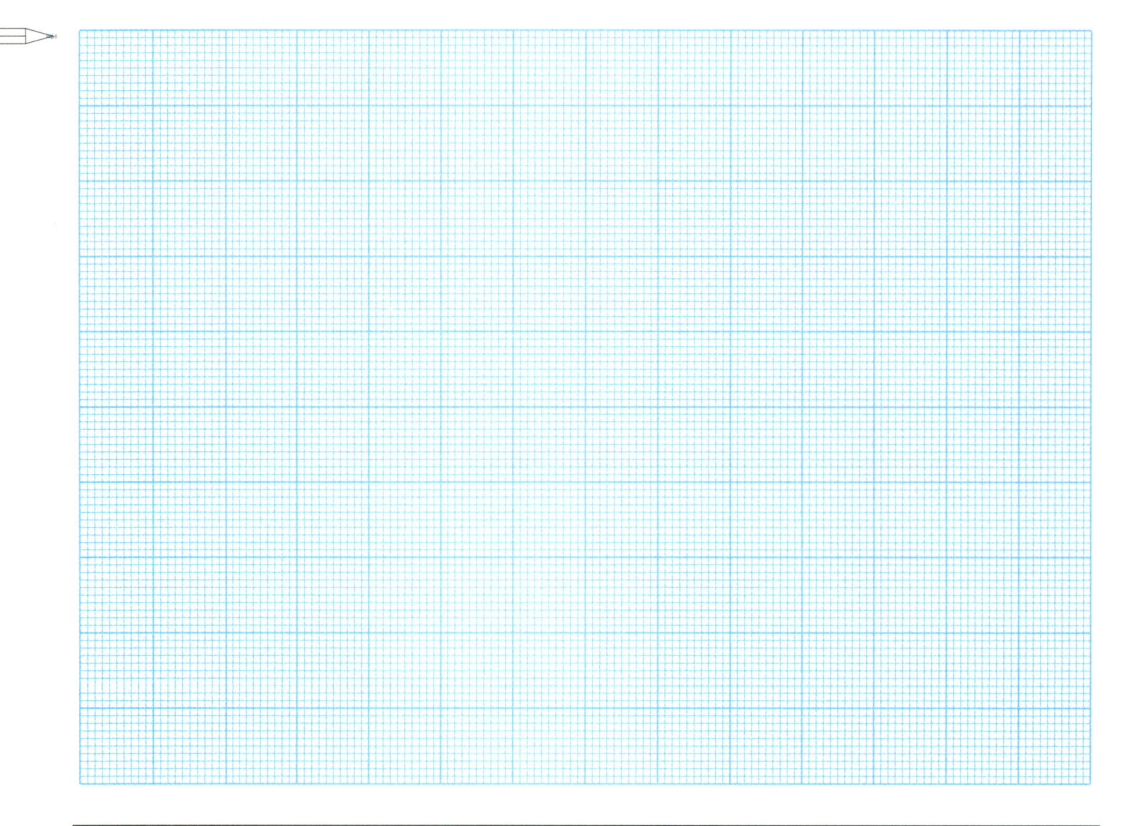

b How are the engine size and the cost related?

Test C

c Draw a line of best fit on your diagram.

d Using this graph, how much would you expect to pay for a car with a 1.3 litre engine?

....

5 A rubber stamp produces this shape:

The shape can be used to make patterns. The pattern shown below has only 2 lines of symmetry.

Using the same shape, sketch another pattern that also has only 2 lines of symmetry.

31

6 Here are the first three diagrams in a series of diagrams.

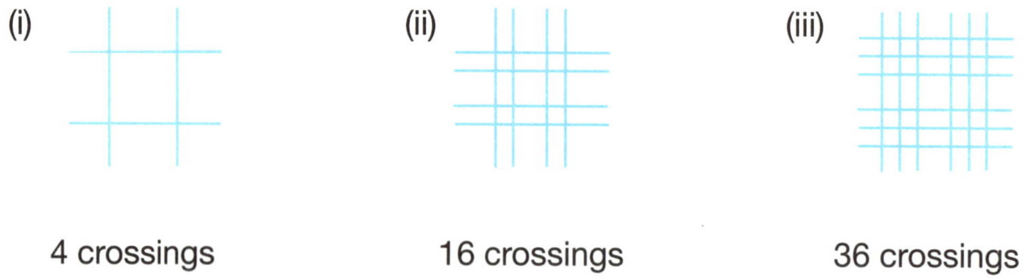

(i) 4 crossings (ii) 16 crossings (iii) 36 crossings

a How many crossings will there be in the fourth diagram?

....

b How many crossings will there be in the tenth diagram?

....

c How many crossings will there be in the *n*th diagram?

....

7a Solve these equations:

(i) $3x + 2 = 17$

....

(ii) $\frac{1}{2}x - 1 = 7$

....

(iii) $2x - 3 = 6 - x$

....

b Solve these inequalities:

(i) 3x + 2 < 17

(ii) 2 − x ≤ 5

8 Michael saves buttons in a tin, in case he needs to replace one on a shirt. He has 12 white buttons, 6 green buttons and 2 brown buttons. Michael takes a button from the tin without looking.

a What is the probability that it is green?

b What is the probability that it is either green or brown?

c Some of the buttons have two holes and the others have four holes. The probability of taking a button with two holes is 0.25.

What is the probability of taking a button with four holes?

d Explain why the probability of taking a button that is either white or has two holes may not be 0.6 + 0.25.

9 The number in the circle in each shape is found by adding the numbers in the four squares surrounding it.

a Write the numbers in the circles for the first three shapes.

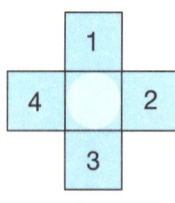

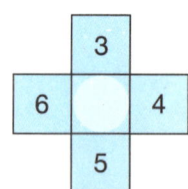

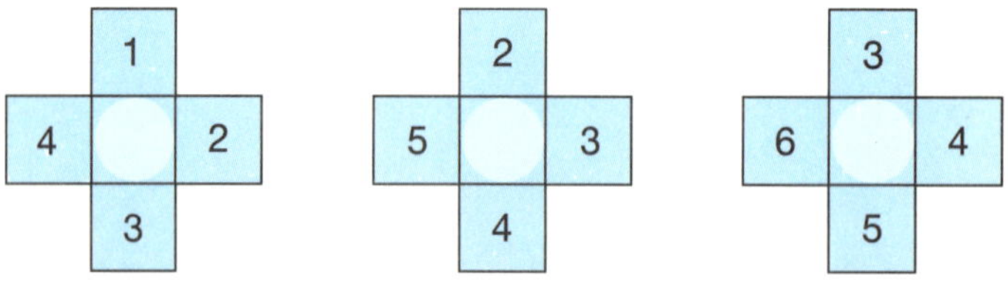

1st: squares 1, 4, 2, 3
2nd: squares 2, 5, 3, 4
3rd: squares 3, 6, 4, 5

b Write down the four numbers that should go in the squares for the *n*th shape. What is the number that should go in the circle for the *n*th shape? Write your answer as simply as possible.

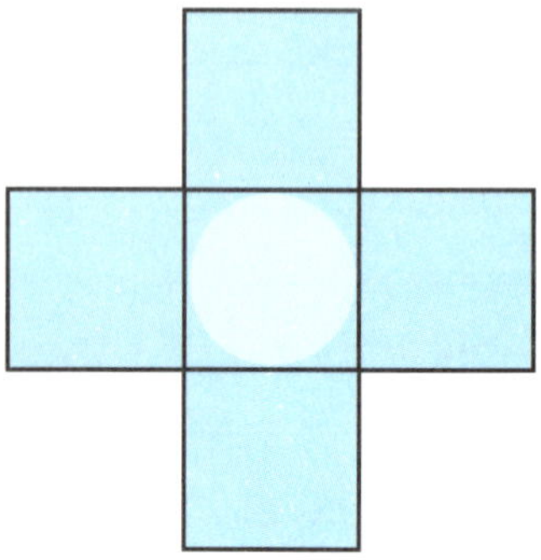

*n*th

10 Cyril worked out: 32.78 ÷ 0.89 = 29.2

a Explain how you know he must be wrong.

b 234 × 0.89 = 208.26   Use this to work out:

(i) 23.4 × 0.89   (ii) 0.0234 × 890   (iii) 20826 ÷ 0.89

34

11 Tasmin is making a garden path using grey and blue paving slabs.

a One way of arranging them is shown below:

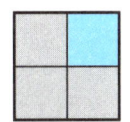

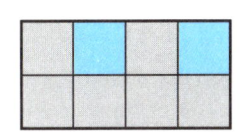

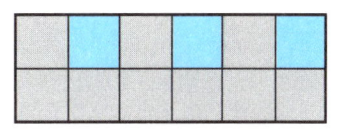

1 blue   2 blue   3 blue

g is the number of grey slabs.
b is the number of blue slabs.

(i) Write down a formula connecting g and b.

....

(ii) How many grey slabs will be needed if 120 blue slabs are used?

....

b Another way of arranging the slabs to form a different border pattern is:

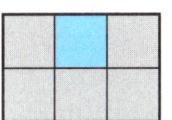

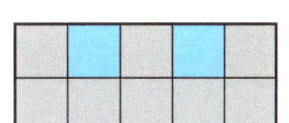

(i) Write down a formula connecting g and b for this pattern.

....

(ii) How many grey slabs will be needed if 100 blue slabs are used?

....

12 Alfred's dad owns a cake shop. The shop is not selling many cakes. Alfred thinks it is because the cakes in his father's shop are too expensive. He conducts a survey to test this. He asks the customers in his father's shop on a Saturday morning about the prices.

a **Why will this not give a fair result? Give two reasons.**

Reason 1: ....

Reason 2: ....

b Here are two of the questions he asked:

A: 'Why do you buy cakes from my father's shop when they are much cheaper elsewhere?'

B: 'Do you think the cakes from this shop represent good value?'

Do you think either of these questions is suitable? Explain.

....

....

....

c **Write two suitable questions he could use.**

....

....

13 Here is a puzzle from a children's book.

A	B	A	B	22
A	B	B	A	22
B	A	B	B	19
A	A	B	A	25
25	22	19	22	

A and B are two unknown numbers. The totals for each row and column are given in the final column and row.

a Explain why $A + 3B = 19$.

b Write down another equation in A and B.

c Solve these two equations to find the values of A and B.

14 This is a scale drawing of a boating lake.
There are small islands at **A** and **B**.

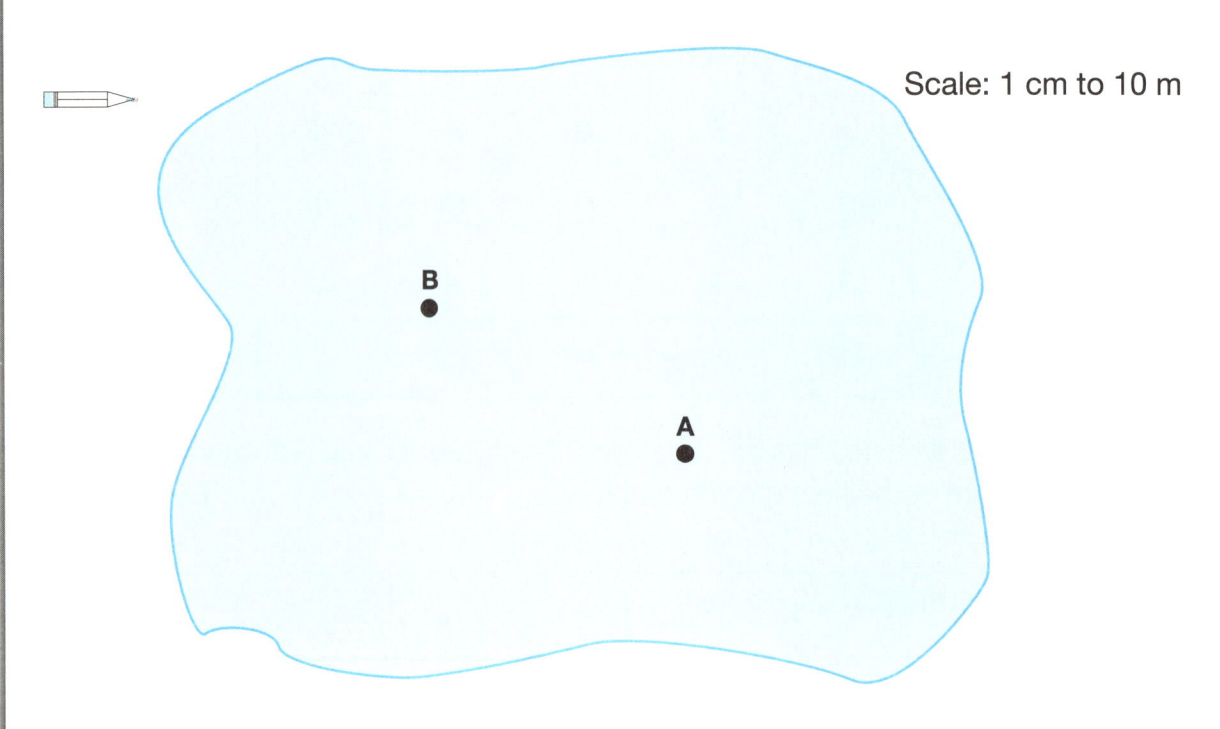

Scale: 1 cm to 10 m

a Frank rows his boat so it is always the same distance from each island.

Draw where Frank's boat goes.

b Maud rows her boat so that it is always 25 m from island **A**.

Draw where Maud's boat goes.

c **Is it possible that they could collide? Explain.**

CALCULATOR CAN BE USED

Test D

TEST D LEVELS 5–7

MARKS

Start ☐ Finish ☐

1 This graph shows the weekly pocket money of students in Fred's class.

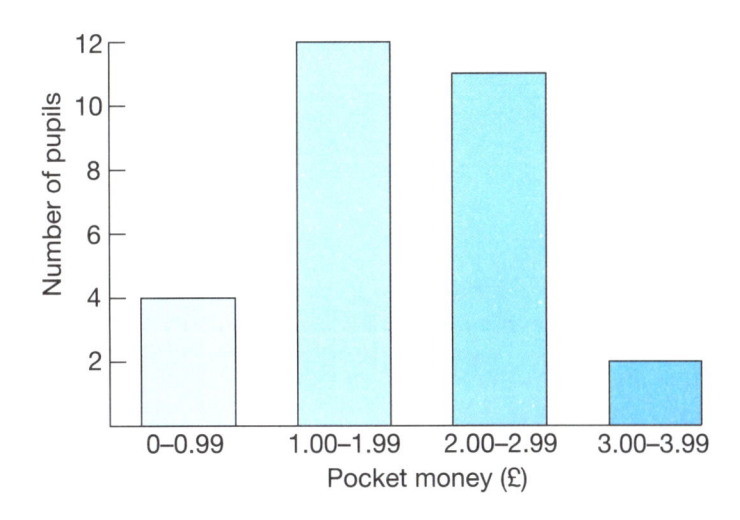

[Bar chart: 0–0.99: 4 pupils; 1.00–1.99: 12 pupils; 2.00–2.99: 11 pupils; 3.00–3.99: 2 pupils. Y-axis: Number of pupils. X-axis: Pocket money (£)]

a How many pupils are there in this class?

....

1 Q1a

b Which is the modal group?

....

1 Q1b

c Here is the data for students in Rachel's class in £s.

2.00	4.00	1.50	7.00	3.00	1.00	2.50	3.50	4.00	4.00
5.00	3.50	2.60	6.00	4.50	1.50	3.00	2.00	3.20	0.50
5.00	3.50	2.50	3.00	4.50	6.00	5.00	2.50	3.00	2.00

Complete the tally chart.

Amount (£)	Tally	Frequency
0.00 – 1.99		
2.00 – 3.99		
4.00 – 5.99		
6.00 – 7.99		

2 Q1c

39

Test D

d | Draw a frequency diagram for this data.

[Frequency diagram axes: Frequency (y-axis), Pocket money (£) (x-axis)]

2 Cargo can travel by lorry or by rail. Scientists have compared the emissions, from each type of transport, for 1 tonne of cargo carried for 1 kilometre.

	Lorry	Rail
Carbon dioxide emission	0.22 kg	0.05 kg
Nitrogen oxides emission	3.6 g	0.22 g
Hydrocarbon emission	0.81 g	0.05 g
Soot	0.27 g	0.03 g

a | What is the total weight of emission from each?

Lorry .... g   Rail .... g

b | What percentage of the total emission from lorries is soot?

....

3 Warren is using a recipe for strawberry ice cream to serve six people.

Strawberry ice cream

600g strawberries
250g sugar
200ml cream
100ml water

a **What weight of strawberries will he need to make ice cream for ten people?**

....

b **How much water will he need?**

....

4 Mrs Jones is planning a school trip to a theme park for the children in her school. 151 children, 5 teachers and 6 parents will be going. The entry cost to the park is £6 per child and £10 per parent. The teachers do not have to pay.

a **Calculate the total cost to enter the park.**

....

b The theme park gives a 15% discount to school parties.

> Calculate the new total entry cost.

c Mrs. Jones will have to hire some coaches to take them to the park. Each coach will cost £156 to hire, and carry 56 people.

> How many coaches will be needed and how much will it cost to hire them?

d
> Find the total cost for the trip.

e This cost is to be shared equally between all the children, the teachers and the adults.

> Find the cost per person.

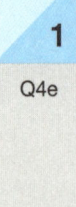

Test D

5

Jane and Ryan go cycling. The wheels on Jane's bike have a diameter of 51 cm.

a What is the circumference of a wheel on Jane's bike? Give your answer in metres.

....

b How many times will the wheel go round when she rides 1600 m?

....

c The diameter of a wheel on Ryan's bike is 66 cm.

How many times will the wheel on his bike go round in 1600 m?

....

6 Find the value of $\dfrac{5.72^2 - 3.16^2}{4.2(16.4 + 0.85)}$ as accurately as you can.

....

7

> **BOYDS BANK** – *The Lending Bank*
>
> **From Monday to Friday**
> **10 to 4**
>
> Every 2 minutes
> we lend someone,
> somewhere, some money!

a How many people will the bank lend money to each day?

b Assume that the 'working week' is Monday to Friday.

How many people are given loans each working week?

c If a year is 50 working weeks long, how many people are given loans each year?

8 The diagram shows a plastic cover used by gardeners to protect their plants. The ends are semi-circles and the whole shape is a half cylinder.

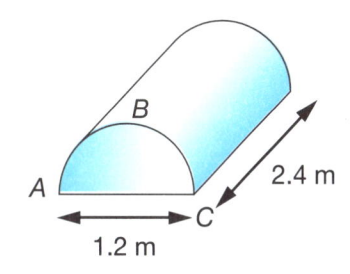

a What is the length of the semicircle ABC?

b Calculate the area of plastic needed for the cover.

c Calculate the volume of air enclosed by the cover.

9 Mary bought a new car yesterday for £12 650. She read in a magazine that the car will lose 25% of its value in the first year.

a How much will the car be worth after one year?

£ ....

b It also said in the magazine that the car will lose 25% of its value every year. Mary thought this meant that it will be worth nothing after four years.

Explain why she is wrong.

....

c How much will the car be worth after four years if the magazine is right?

£ ....

Test D

10 The diameter of a table tennis ball is 4 cm. Table tennis balls are sold in cylindrical tubes each containing 3 balls.

Explain how you would find:

a the radius of the tube.

....

b the length of the tube.

....

Calculate:

c the total volume inside the tube.

....

d the total area of plastic used to make a tube, including both ends.

....

TEST D
LEVELS 5–7

MARKS

11 Sodapeps make canned drinks. Each can contains 440 ml. A new can is made to hold 500 ml.

a **What is the percentage increase in the size of can?**

[1] Q11a

....

b On top of the new can is printed '13.5% more'.

Is this correct? Explain your answer.

[1] Q11b

....

c The measurement 440 ml is correct to the nearest millilitre.

What is the least amount the can could contain?

[1] Q11c

.... ml

12 Marker buoys **A**, **B**, **C** and **D** are placed in the shape of a triangle on the sea to mark the turning points for a speed boat race. **A** is the start, **B** is 50 km East of **A**, **C** is 35 km North of **A**, and **D** is West of **A** and 40 km from **C**.

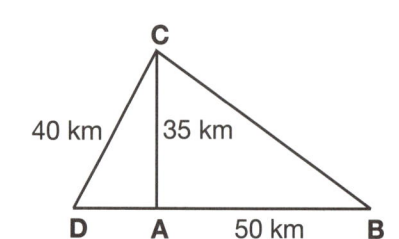

```
           C
          /|\
    40 km/ |35 km\
        /  |      \
       D   A  50 km  B
```

a **Use Pythagoras' theorem to calculate the total distance round the course from A to B, C, D and back to A.**

[4] Q12a

....

....

48

b | Calculate the time for a speed boat to complete the course at an average speed of 40 km per hour.

....

13

Country	Area (in km²)	1968 Population (in millions)	1994 Population (in millions)
Germany	356 000	77.26	85.3
United Kingdom	243 000	55.3	57.3

a | Between 1968 and 1994 which country had the greater percentage increase in population? Show your working.

....

....

b | In 1994, which country had the greater number of people per square kilometre? Show your working.

....

....

14 One solution of the quadratic equation:

$$x^2 - 3x + 1 = 0$$

is close to 1.

a Find this solution correct to two decimal places.

b Find the other solution, also correct to two decimal places.

Mental Test

Ask a friend or a parent to detach page 71 and read the questions to you.
Each question will be read twice and you then have 10 seconds to complete your answer.

You only need a pen or pencil. **You must not use a calculator, ruler or any other geometric instruments.**

Write your answers on the lines below.

1 ....

2 .... °C

3 ....

4 ....

5 .... cm

6 ....

A ———————————— B

7 .... cm

8 ....

9 .... litres

10 ....

11 ....

12 ....

13 .... g

14 ....

15 £ ....

16 ....

17 ....

18 ....

19 .... degrees

20 ....

Answers

HOW TO MARK THE QUESTIONS

When marking your test remember the answers given are sample answers. You must look at your answers and judge whether they deserve credit. Award the mark if the answer deserves credit. Although you should always try to spell words accurately, do not mark any answer wrong because the words are misspelt.

In the answers below, the calculation is often given as well as the answer. Sometimes the method earns credit (e.g. Question 3 in Test B), but other times only the answer itself earns credit (e.g. Question 1d in Test B). In these cases, the working out has been provided to help you understand how to arrive at the correct answer.

When you go through the answers, try to work out where you have gone wrong. Make a note of the key points, so that you will remember them next time.

Only count the marks you scored in one hour on each test. Enter your marks for each test on the Marking Grid on page 74, and then work out your level of achievement on these tests on page 73.

TEST A Pages 2–16

1   B: Yes, C: no, D: yes, E: no, F: yes   *2 marks*
                                                                        Total 2 marks

> **Examiner's tip**
>
> If you made one mistake you would score one mark. The shapes must be the same size and shape to be congruent.

2a   White 8, red 13, blue 9, green 6   *2 marks*

b

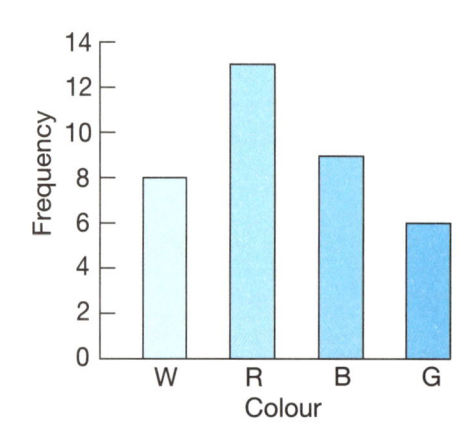

2 marks

c   Blue; it is the largest angle.   *2 marks*
                                                                        Total 6 marks

Test A Answers

Examiner's tip
If you make one mistake in part **a** you will score one mark, also in part **b**. You will get full marks if the height of the bars is consistent with your previous answers.

3a   1, 4, 9, 16, 25   *All required*   1 mark
b   36 in row 4, 49 in row 5   *Both required*   1 mark
Total 2 marks

Examiner's tip
Notice that the row number is one more than the tens digit.

4   (62 ÷ 2) × 5 = 155 = £1.55   1 mark
Total 1 mark

Examiner's tip
You could leave the answer in pence but it is more usual to give it in £s.

5a (i)   9, 11   1 mark
  (ii)   10, 12   1 mark
 (iii)   19, 23   1 mark
b   Each term in pattern (iii) is the sum of the two corresponding terms in patterns (i) and (ii).   1 mark
Total 4 marks

Examiner's tip
Alternative words are acceptable in part **b**, so long as your answer means the same!

6a   1556 − 1030 = 5 hours 26 minutes   1 mark
b   1650 + 1 hour 14 minutes = 1804   1 mark
Total 2 marks

Examiner's tip
If you add 1650 to 114 you get 1764, which is not a time on the 24-hour clock! Remember there are 60 minutes in an hour, not 100.

Test A Answers

7

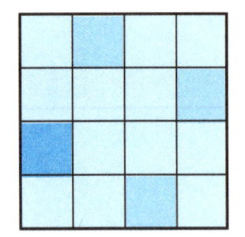

a

b

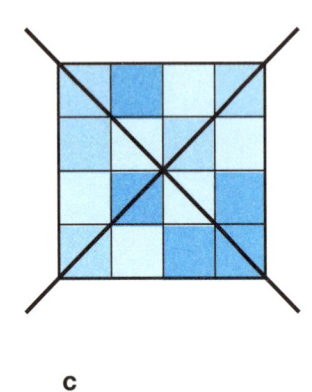

c

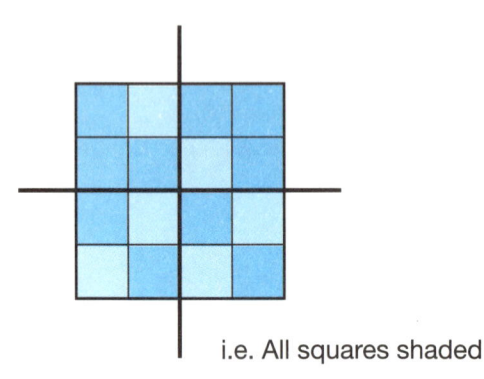

d i.e. All squares shaded

One mark for each diagram: 4 marks
Total 4 marks

Examiner's tip

There is one mark for each completely correct diagram.

8 Two right-angled triangles with sides 3 cm, 4 cm, 5 cm added to the diagram, one on each side.

3 marks
Total 3 marks

Examiner's tip

Ask someone to check that the lengths you have drawn are correct. It does not matter which sides of the net you have drawn the triangles on, as long as they are on opposite sides of the net and each triangle has sides of 3 cm, 4 cm, 5 cm. It should be possible to make up the 3-D wedge from the net.

9a $\frac{9}{20}$

1 mark

b Number not grey = 15

Probability $\frac{15}{20} = \frac{3}{4}$

1 mark
Total 2 marks

Examiner's tip

The answer for a probability should be a fraction, decimal or percentage, not a ratio or expression such as '9 out of 20'.

Test A Answers

10   28 rounded to 30   *1 mark*
420 rounded to 400 and 400 × 30 = 12 000   *1 mark*
Total 2 marks

Examiner's tip
There is often more than one way to approximate a calculation but in this case you were given the answer!

11   1.457, 15.47, 145.7, 154.7, 174.5, 1457.0   *2 marks*
Total 2 marks

Examiner's tip
Look carefully at the position of the decimal points. If you make only one error you will still score one mark.

12 $A = 16, B = 288, C = 324, D = 1296$ *One mark for each number: 4 marks*
Total 4 marks

Examiner's tip
You can find D either along the row by doubling or down the column by multiplying by 3.

13a

3rd digit	4th digit
1	2
1	5
2	1
2	5
5	1
5	2

2 marks

b $\frac{1}{6}$ *1 mark*
Total 3 marks

Examiner's tip
It is easier if you are systematic in listing all the combinations. If you make just one error in the table you will still score one mark.

14a a is 58°, corresponding (or F-) angles   *2 marks*
b $c = a = 58°$ as is isosceles triangle
$b = 64°$ from the angle sum of a triangle ($a + b + c = 180°$)
d is 64°, the same as b, alternate (or Z-) angles   *2 marks*
Total 4 marks

Examiner's tip
It is important to give clear reasons. You can work out d from the angles on a straight line.

Test A Answers

15a Between 200 and 250 grams or $\frac{1}{4}$ kg *1 mark*

b
```
   27
  ×18
  ───
  270
  216
  ───
  486
```
= £4.86 *2 marks*

c 300 ÷ 2.5 = 120 inches *1 mark*

d 275 ÷ 15 = 18.3, 18 whole tiles *2 marks*

Total 6 marks

Examiner's tip

To answer part **a** you need to remember that one kilogram is just over two pounds. In part **b** the answer should be in pounds. In part **c** it is useful to notice that 2.5 is half of 5 and there are 20 '5's in each 100. A short method in part **d** comes from seeing that 20 tiles gives 300 cm, just too big.

16a Drawing with two angles and two lengths correct *4 marks*

b 62 mm on plan, 310 m on the field *1 mark*

Total 5 marks

Examiner's tip

Ask someone to check your measurements. The angles should be within 1° and the lengths within 1 mm of 46 mm and 58 mm. If you have made an error, you may still get the last mark if you convert your measurement correctly to metres.

17a (2, 3, 5, 7), 11, 13, 17, (19), 23, 29 *1 mark*

b (i) $3x$, $3x - 3$ *1 mark*

(ii) $x + 3x + 3x - 3 = 46$ or $7x - 3 = 46$ *1 mark*

(iii) $7x = 49$, $x = 7$ *1 mark*

The other numbers are 21 and 18. *1 mark*

Total 5 marks

Examiner's tip

To score all the marks you must write down all the steps, even if you can solve the problem in your head!

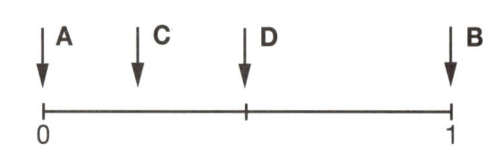

18 A C D B on number line from 0 to 1 *3 marks*

Total 3 marks

Examiner's tip

You need to consider the four possible combinations to answer this question. There is one mark for each correct answer to **B**, **C** and **D**.

TEST TOTAL 60 MARKS

Test B Answers

TEST B *Pages 17–27*

1a 6 × 17p = 102p = £1.02 — *1 mark*
b Bill total = £6.59
Change = £3.41 — *1 mark*
c $\frac{25}{40} = \frac{5}{8}$ — *1 mark*
d 40 − 25 = 15
$\frac{15}{40} \times 100 = 37.5\%$ — *1 mark*
Total 4 marks

Examiner's tip

The fraction in part **c** is better given in its lowest terms, although any equivalent fraction is correct. For part **d**, remember it is how much she saved.

2a 22°C — *1 mark*
b Circumference of flower bed = 2 × π × 5 — *1 mark*
4 plants in each metre
Number of plants = 2 × π × 5 × 4 = 125.66... — *1 mark*
125 or 126 plants needed. — *1 mark*
Total 4 marks

Examiner's tip

The formula for the circumference of a circle will be given at the front of a test paper. Either answer is acceptable for part **b**. You cannot have 0.66 of a plant – it will not grow!

3 $\frac{36 - 24.5}{24.5} \times 100 = 46.9\%$ — *2 marks*
Total 2 marks

Examiner's tip

There is one mark for attempting the correct calculation and one for the right answer.

4a 90° — *1 mark*
b Angles in pie chart: carbohydrate 216°, fat 90°, protein 54° — *2 marks*
Total 3 marks

Examiner's tip

If one angle is right in part **b** you will score one mark. You can draw the angles with an angle measurer (protractor) in degrees or with a pie chart scale in per cent.

Test B Answers

5	$1000 \div 240 = 4.167$	1 mark
	5 amp fuse required.	1 mark
		Total 2 marks

Examiner's tip
The fuse rating must be higher than the current.

6a	$\frac{12}{16} = \frac{3}{4}$	1 mark
b	$\frac{3}{16} \times 100 = 18.75\%$	1 mark
c	$2 \times \frac{3}{12} = 0.5$ m^3	1 mark
		Total 3 marks

Examiner's tip
The fraction and the percentage in parts **a** and **b** are based on the total amount but in **c** you are only concerned with the proportions of sand and cement.

7	$30.48 \div 3.52 = 8.659...$	1 mark
	8 Metros will fit.	1 mark
		Total 2 marks

Examiner's tip
A ninth Metro will make it longer than the large car.

8a	**(i)**	A straight line through $(0, -1)$ and $(\frac{1}{2}, 0)$.	2 marks
	(ii)	A straight line through $(0, 3)$ and $(3, 0)$.	2 marks
b		$x = 1.3, y = 1.7$	1 mark
			Total 5 marks

Examiner's tip
Your lines should extend further than the points mentioned. If you have drawn the lines carefully you should be able to be this accurate in reading the co-ordinates.

9a	$\frac{17.5}{100} \times 364 = £63.70$	1 mark
b	$364 + 63.70 = £427.70$	1 mark
		Total 2 marks

Examiner's tip
The answer to **b** can be obtained by multiplying the price without VAT by 1.175.

Test B Answers

10   2.25 and 17.75 are correct to 2 decimal places.   *4 marks*
Total 4 marks

Examiner's tip

The numbers are 2.2540333... and 17.7459666... but you are not expected to spend as long as that in finding them! Make sure you do your trials systematically, always trying to get nearer the result, and write down your working.

11a   25 000 × £0.35 = £8 750   *1 mark*
  b   25 000 × 0.13 = 3250 litres   *1 mark*
  c   3250 × £0.569 = £1849.25   *1 mark*
Total 3 marks

Examiner's tip

It is a good idea to change pence to £s before calculating.

12   134 × 0.85 = £113.90
       134 − 20 = £114, Snappers is cheaper   *2 marks*
Total 2 marks

Examiner's tip

It is more efficient to find 85% of the original price than to find 15% and subtract. Finding 85% is the same as multiplying by 0.85.

13a   A square, length of side 5 units   *2 marks*
  b   FORWARD 3
        TURN RIGHT 90°
        FORWARD 7
        TURN RIGHT 90°
        FORWARD 3
        TURN RIGHT 90°
        FORWARD 7   *2 marks*
Total 4 marks

Examiner's tip

You must give the size of the square, not only its shape. In part **b** you can do the 7 before the 3 or go the other way round, turning LEFT rather than RIGHT. If you make one mistake, you will score 1 mark.

14a   83 + 86 + 98 + 87 + 96 = 450
        450 ÷ 5 = 90   *1 mark*
  b   Highest is 98, lowest is 83 so range is 98 − 83 = 15   *1 mark*
  c   Agree: Ruth has higher mean.   *1 mark*
        Disagree: Joan has bigger range and may have a higher score in one test.   *1 mark*
Total 4 marks

Examiner's tip

Ruth has the higher mean and the smaller range. Therefore her performance is more consistent.

Test B Answers

15   Total = 96 942, % bricks = $\frac{27\,696}{96\,942} \times 100 = 28.569...\%$ *2 marks*
Total 2 marks

Examiner's tip
There is one mark for a correct method. 28.6% is a reasonable answer to this problem.

16 a $5 \times 18 + 15 \times 11 = 255$ m²   *2 marks*
  b $\frac{11 \times 11}{255} \times 100 = 47.5\%$ *2 marks*
Total 4 marks

Examiner's tip
The garden can be divided into rectangles to find the area in other ways, $20 \times 11 + 7 \times 5$ for instance. Do not forget the units in part **a**.

17   £1800 $\times \frac{12}{45}$ = £480   *2 marks*
Total 2 marks

Examiner's tip
You would score one mark here if you knew that you must multiply by the fraction but made a mistake in doing it.

18   50 coins in £25   *1 mark*
         50 $\times$ 13.5 g = 675 g = 0.675 kg   *1 mark*
Total 2 marks

Examiner's tip
Remember there are 1000 g in a kilogram.

19 a   £66 000   *1 mark*
 b(i)   new cost of materials   £24 150   *1 mark*
          new cost of wages   £43 200   *1 mark*
          new overheads   £5250   *1 mark*
          new total cost   £72 600   *1 mark*

   (ii)   percentage increase = $\frac{72\,600 - 66\,000}{66\,000} \times 100\% = 10\%$ *1 mark*

Total 6 marks

Examiner's tip
The percentage increase is not 15% + 5% + 8%. You need to work out the new individual costs in order to find the new total.

TEST TOTAL 60 MARKS

Test C Answers

TEST C *Pages 28–38*

1a
```
      14
17)254
    17
    ──
    84
    68
    ──
    16
```
15 cans needed *2 marks*

b $\frac{1}{17} \times 3 = 0.18$ litres *2 marks*

c largest area = 254.5 m²   smallest area = 253.5 m² *2 marks*

Total 6 marks

Examiner's tip

Remember to show clearly how you did the calculation in part **a**. In part **b**, 15 cans needed but only $14\frac{16}{17}$ cans are used, so $\frac{1}{17}$ can is not used. One can holds 3 litres so $\frac{3}{17}$ litres of paint is not used.

2

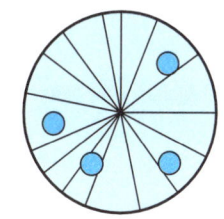

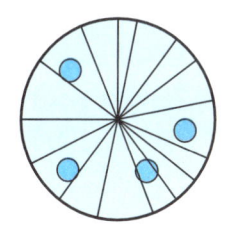

2 marks
Total 2 marks

Examiner's tip

If two are right you will score one mark. You can use a tracing if it helps.

3a $2h$ *1 mark*
b $3g + h$ *1 mark*
c $6g$ *1 mark*
d $2g + 4h$ *1 mark*

Total 4 marks

Examiner's tip

There is one mark for each part. The perimeter is only round the outside.

Test C Answers

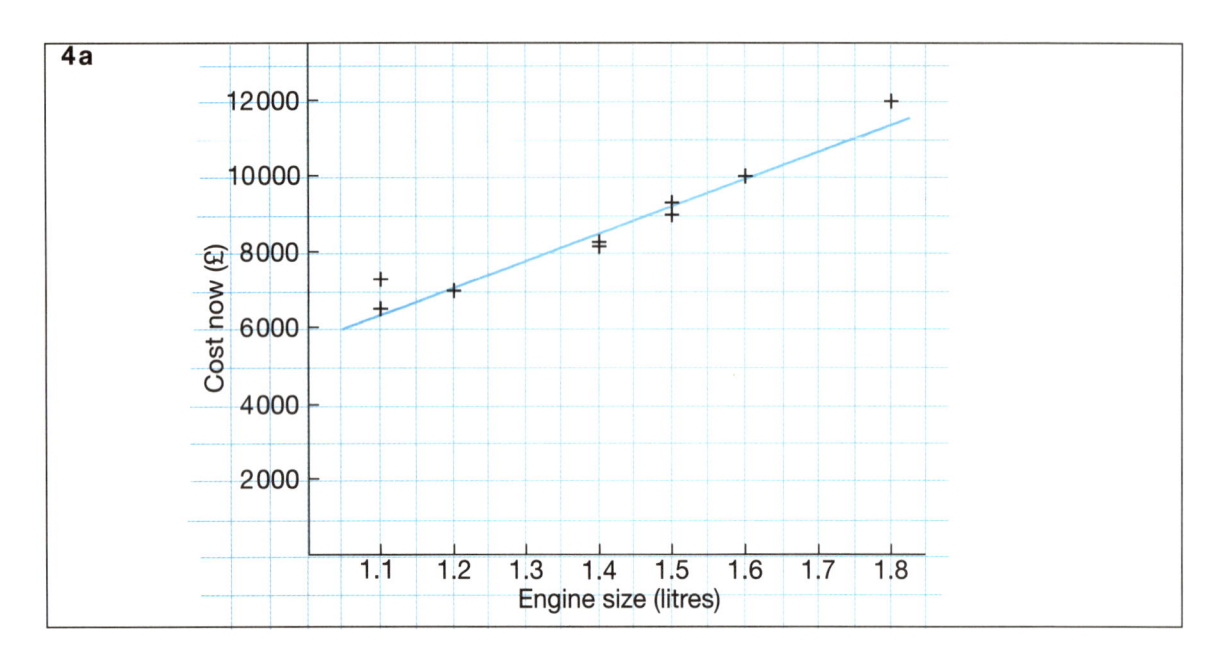

4a

[Graph: Cost now (£) vs Engine size (litres), with scatter points and line of best fit from approximately (1.1, 6000) to (1.8, 11500)]

3 marks

b The larger the engine the greater the cost. — *1 mark*
c Line of best fit (on graph) — *1 mark*
d Between £7500 and £8000 — *1 mark*

Total 6 marks

Examiner's tip

One mark in part **a** will be for drawing suitable axes and labelling them. You could use the term 'correlation' in answering part **b**. In this case it is 'positive correlation'.

5

[Shape with two lines of symmetry]

2 marks
Total 2 marks

Examiner's tip

The only limit to the number of shapes you can draw is the size of the paper. This is a simple one that has only two lines of symmetry, as required.

6a 64 — *1 mark*
b 400 — *1 mark*
c $4n^2$ or $(2n)^2$ — *1 mark*

Total 3 marks

Examiner's tip

Notice that $2n^2$ is WRONG!

Test C Answers

7 a (i) $3x = 15$, $x = 5$ — *1 mark*
  (ii) $\frac{1}{2}x = 8$, $x = 16$ — *1 mark*
  (iii) $3x - 3 = 6$, $3x = 9$, $x = 3$ — *2 marks*

  b (i) $3x < 17 - 2$, $3x < 15$, $x < 5$ — *1 mark*
   (ii) $2 - 5 \leq x$, $x \geq -3$ — *1 mark*
   Total 6 marks

Examiner's tip
Care is needed with the direction of the sign in part **b(ii)**.

8 a $\frac{6}{20} = \frac{3}{10}$ — *1 mark*

b $\frac{3}{10} + \frac{1}{10} = \frac{4}{10} = \frac{2}{5}$ — *1 mark*

c $1 - 0.25 = 0.75$ — *1 mark*
d Some white buttons may also have two holes — *2 marks*
Total 5 marks

Examiner's tip
Notice that it was possible to add the probabilities in part **b** as no button was both green and brown. In part **d** however, the two outcomes are not mutually exclusive, or at least you do not know that they are. You can of course work out part **b** by adding the numbers of green and brown buttons and then dividing by 20.

9 a 10, 14, 18 — *1 mark*
b (Clockwise from top) n, $n + 1$, $n + 2$, $n + 3$, centre $4n + 6$ — *2 marks*
Total 3 marks

Examiner's tip
In part **b** there is one mark for the numbers in the squares and one mark for the number in the circle.

10 a 32.78 is divided by a number smaller than 1, so the answer must be bigger than 32.78. — *1 mark*
  b (i) 20.826
   (ii) 20.826
   (iii) 23 400 — *3 marks*
   Total 4 marks

Examiner's tip
Remember that multiplying by 10 moves the digits one place left (decimal point one place right), so that in part **b(ii)** 0.0234 is $234 \div 10\,000$ and 890 is 89×10, giving the result $20\,826 \div 1000$.

Test C Answers

11 a (i) $g = 3b$ — 1 mark
(ii) $3 \times 120 = 360$ — 1 mark
b (i) $g = 3b + 2$ — 1 mark
(ii) $3 \times 100 + 2 = 302$ — 1 mark
Total 4 marks

Examiner's tip

The formula $g = 5b$ only works for the first pattern in part **b**!

12 a Saturday is not typical of the days in the week. — 1 mark
Needs to ask people who do not use the shop. — 1 mark
b A: No, it is a leading question. — 1 mark
B: No, it is asked in the shop so customers are likely to say 'Yes'. — 1 mark
c 'Do you ever buy cakes?' — 1 mark
'How much do you spend on cakes each week?' — 1 mark
Total 6 marks

Examiner's tip

There are many other questions you could write, e.g. 'Do you buy cakes from other shops?', 'Where do you buy cakes?', 'Do you buy cakes at my father's shop?'.

13 a $A + 3B = 19$ comes from the third row or the third column — 1 mark
b $3A + B = 25$ or $2A + 2B = 22$ — 1 mark
c $3A + 9B = 57$ (= 3 × (**a**))
$3A + B = 25$ — 1 mark
Subtract $8B = 32$ — 1 mark
$B = 4, A = 7$ — 1 mark
Total 5 marks

Examiner's tip

You could have used the other equation instead of either of these. Try it again to check it gives the same result!

14 a A straight line bisecting **AB** at right angles. — 1 mark
b A circle centre **A** radius 2.5 cm. — 2 marks
c Yes, the paths cross at two points. — 1 mark
Total 4 marks

Examiner's tip

The position of Frank's boat will always form an isosceles triangle with **A** and **B**.

TEST TOTAL 60 MARKS

Test D Answers

TEST D *Pages 39–50*

1a 29 — *1 mark*
b £1.00 – £1.99 — *1 mark*
c Frequencies: 4, 15, 8, 3 — *2 marks*
d — *2 marks*

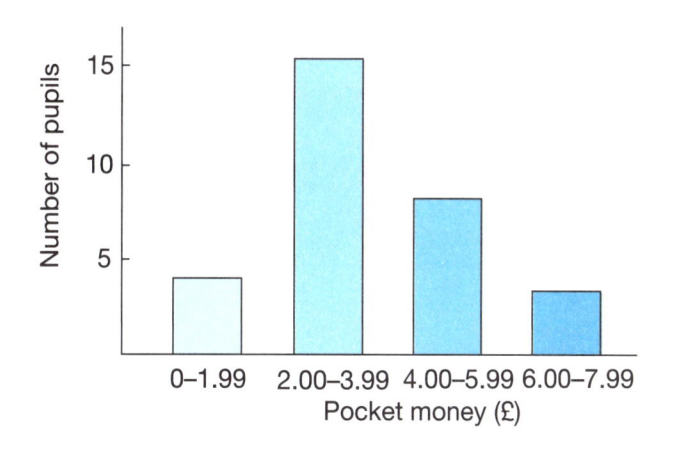

[Bar chart showing Number of pupils vs Pocket money (£): 0–1.99: 4, 2.00–3.99: 15, 4.00–5.99: 8, 6.00–7.99: 3]

Total 6 marks

Examiner's tip

You will lose one mark for an error in the tally in part **c** but full marks would be given for a bar chart which is correct for your frequencies.

2a Lorry 224.68 g   Rail 50.3 g — *2 marks*
b $\frac{0.27}{224.68} \times 100\% = 0.12\%$ — *1 mark*

Total 3 marks

Examiner's tip

The original data does not justify more figures in the answer to part **b**. Remember to change kg to g before you start.

3a $600 \times \frac{10}{6} = 1000$ g or 1 kg — *1 mark*
b $100 \times \frac{10}{6} = 166.66...$ or 170 ml — *1 mark*

Total 2 marks

Examiner's tip

166.66... is not a sensible answer as you would not try to be so accurate when cooking. However, you would not lose the mark if you answered 166.66... in this case.

Test D Answers

4a	£151 × 6 + 6 × 10 = £966	*1 mark*
b	£966 × 0.85 = £821.10	*1 mark*
c	162 ÷ 56 = 2.8... 3 coaches needed	*1 mark*
	Cost = £156 × 3 = £468	*1 mark*
d	£1289.10	*1 mark*
e	£1289.10 ÷ 162 = £7.96	*1 mark*
		Total 6 marks

Examiner's tip

It is important to check your work since later answers depend on earlier ones. However you will get some marks if you make a mistake but later methods are right. The answer to part **e** has been rounded to the nearest penny. A further question could have been 'How much should she charge?', and a sensible answer would be £8, as it is much easier to collect!

5a	2 × π × 0.255 = 1.60... m	*2 marks*
b	1600 ÷ 1.60... = 998.6 or 999 or 1000	*2 marks*
c	998.6... × $\frac{51}{66}$ = 771.66... or 772 or 770	*2 marks*
		Total 6 marks

Examiner's tip

If you do not understand inverse proportion, part **c** can be done in a similar way to parts **a** and **b**. Given the measurements and nature of the problem, more figures are not justified.

6	0.313772256	*1 mark*
		Total 1 mark

Examiner's tip

In this sort of question write down all the digits in your calculator display. Yours may not have as many as this. Remember to use brackets or add the 16.4 to 0.85 before dividing it into the previous result.

7a	6 × 30 = 180	*1 mark*
b	180 × 5 = 900	*1 mark*
c	900 × 50 = 45 000	*1 mark*
		Total 3 marks

Examiner's tip

In part **a** there are 30 people an hour and the bank is open for 6 hours. Parts **b** and **c** just follow on.

Test D Answers

8a	$\frac{1}{2} \times 2 \times \pi \times 0.6 = 1.88...$ m		*1 mark*
b	$1.88... \times 2.4$		*1 mark*
	$+ 2 \times \frac{1}{2} \times \pi \times 0.6^2$		*1 mark*
	$= 5.65$ m²		*1 mark*
c	$\frac{1}{2} \times \pi \times 0.6^2 \times 2.4 = 1.36$ m³		*2 marks*
			Total 6 marks

Examiner's tip

The formulae you need will be at the front of a test paper. Notice the marks available for your method and the rounding of the answers to no more figures than the data. Make sure you do not round an answer which you need to use in a later calculation, as in part **a**.

9a	$12\,650 \times 0.75 = £9487.50$	*1 mark*
b	Amount lost is based on the start value each year.	*1 mark*
c	$12\,650 \times 0.75 \times 0.75 \times 0.75 \times 0.75 = £4002.54$	*1 mark*
		Total 3 marks

Examiner's tip

It is easier to multiply by 0.75 than to have to take off 25%!

10a	Half the diameter of a ball	*1 mark*
b	3 times the diameter of a ball	*1 mark*
c	$\pi \times 2^2 \times 12 = 150.8$ cm³	*2 marks*
d	$2 \times \pi \times 2^2 + 2 \times \pi \times 2 \times 12 = 175.9$ cm²	*2 marks*
		Total 6 marks

Examiner's tip

Don't forget there are two ends to include in part **d**.

11a	$\frac{500 - 440}{440} \times 100 = 13.64\%$	*1 mark*
b	True. It is slightly more than 13.5%.	*1 mark*
c	439.5 ml	*1 mark*
		Total 3 marks

Examiner's tip

Remember % changes are calculated as actual change divided by original amount.

Test D Answers

12a $BC^2 = 35^2 + 50^2$ — *1 mark*
$BC = \sqrt{3725} = 61.0...$ — *1 mark*
$AD = \sqrt{(40^2 - 35^2)} = \sqrt{375} = 19.36...$ — *1 mark*
Length of course = 50 + 61.0... + 40 + 19.36... = 170.4 km — *1 mark*
b 170.4 ÷ 40 = 4.26 ... = 4 hours 16 minutes — *1 mark*
Total 5 marks

Examiner's tip

The formula for Pythagoras' theorem will be at the front of a Key Stage 3 test paper. Don't round the answers until you get to the final one as you may get an inaccurate answer. The time is given to the nearest minute.

13a Germany: $\frac{85.3 - 77.26}{77.26} \times 100 = 10.4\%$ — *1 mark*

UK: $\frac{57.3 - 55.3}{55.3} \times 100 = 3.6\%$ — *1 mark*

Germany had greater % increase.

b Germany: $\frac{85\,300\,000}{356\,000} = 239.6$ — *1 mark*

UK: $\frac{57\,300\,000}{243\,000} = 235.8$ — *1 mark*

Germany had the greater number.

Total 4 marks

Examiner's tip

Percentage increase is calculated using actual increase divided by original amounts.

14a 0.38 — *3 marks*
b 2.62 — *3 marks*
Total 6 marks

Examiner's tip

Use 'trial and improvement'. Work out the value of $x^2 - 3x + 1$ when $x = 1$. This gives −1. Try 0.5. This gives − 0.25 which is nearer to 0 which is the target. Continue systematically and write down your trials as they will score marks as well as the answer. In part **b** you have to find the starting number for yourself. If you have not obtained these answers, you may still get part marks. For both **a** and **b**, one mark is awarded for a trial worked out and another mark is awarded for a trial with a value nearer to the solution.

TEST TOTAL 60 MARKS

Mental Test Answers

1	20 305	11	11
2	7	12	2000
3	16.5	13	300
4	1	14	40
5	600	15	25
6	750	16	0.6
7	5 or 6	17	30
8	150	18	$5x$
9	20	19	80
10	28	20	120

Examiner's tip

You must listen carefully. 'Sixty' can sound like 'sixteen' if you are not concentrating. Look for short methods, for example, in question 12, multiplying by 25 is the same as multiplying by 100 and dividing by 4. To answer question 11 you should find the perfect squares nearest to 130. The answer is the square root of the one that is nearer. Ten seconds may not sound very long but, with practice, you should be able to answer questions like this in that time in your head. To get some more practice, ask someone to make up other questions like these, but with different numbers. Your score should soon improve – your target is to get them all right!

Mental Test Questions

INSTRUCTIONS

Detach this page from the book.
Read each question, exactly as printed, twice.
Allow 10 seconds for each answer to be written down (on page 51).

1   Write in figures twenty thousand three hundred and five.
2   The temperature this morning was minus two degrees. Now it is five degrees. How much has the temperature gone up?
3   Divide one hundred and sixty-five by ten.
4   Add seven to negative six.
5   The length of a room is six metres. How many centimetres is this?
6   Multiply seven point five by a hundred.
7   Estimate the length of line AB in centimetres.
8   What is sixty percent of two hundred and fifty?
9   A tank holds twenty thousand millilitres. How many litres is this?
10 Find two-thirds of forty-two.
11 What is the square root of one hundred and thirty to the nearest whole number?
12 Multiply twenty-five by eighty.
13 A loaf of bread weights point three kilograms. How many grams is this?
14 What is twelve thousand divided by three hundred?
15 Janet and John share forty pounds in the ratio five to three. How much is the larger share?
16 Write three-fifths as a decimal.
17 Multiply point nought three by a thousand.
18 Write as simply as possible: three x minus four x plus six x.
19 Two angles of a triangle are forty degrees and sixty degrees. What is the third angle?
20 What is twenty-four divided by point two?

Formulae

You might need to use these formulae. For π, use the value of π given on your calculator. If your calculator does not have a π button, use π = 3.142.

AREA

Circle

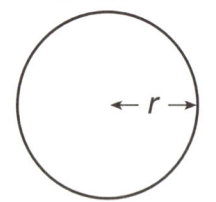

πr^2

Rectangle

length × width

Triangle

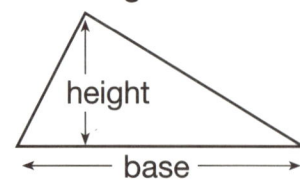

$\dfrac{\text{base} \times \text{height}}{2}$

Parallelogram

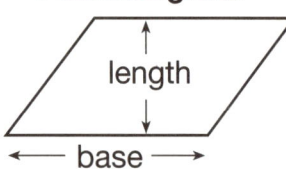

base × height

Trapezium

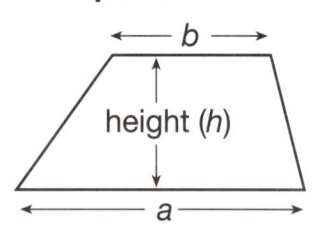

$\dfrac{(a + b)}{2} \times h$

LENGTH

Circle

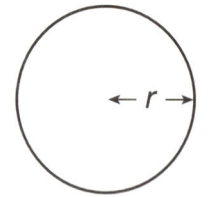

circumference = $2\pi r$

For a right-angled triangle

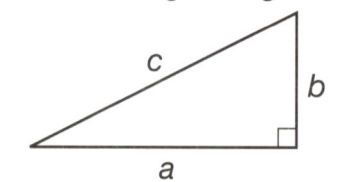

$a^2 + b^2 = c^2$ (Pythagoras' theorem)

VOLUME

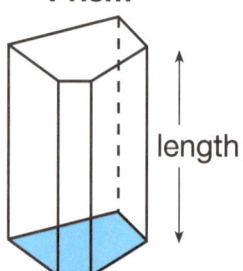

Prism

area of cross-section × length

Determining your level

FINDING YOUR LEVEL IN EACH TEST

When you have completed and marked a test, enter the total number of marks you scored for each question on the Marking Grid overleaf. Then add them up. Using the total for each test, look at the charts below to determine your level for each test.

Test A or Test B

Level 3 or below	Level 4	Level 5	Level 6
up to 16	17–28	29–40	41+

After you have worked out separate levels for Tests A and B, add up your total marks for the two tests. Use this total and the chart below to determine your overall level for Tests A and B — this is your level for Mathematics at this point.

Total for Tests A and B

Level 3 or below	Level 4	Level 5	Level 6
up to 33	34–57	58–81	82+

If your results from Tests A and B indicate that you are working at Level 4 or higher, you should try Tests C and D sometime later. The chart below shows you how to find your level for each of Tests C and D.

Test C or Test D

Level 4 or below	Level 5	Level 6	Level 7 or above
up to 15	16–24	25–42	43+

FINDING YOUR OVERALL LEVEL IN MATHEMATICS

After you have found your level for each test, add up your total marks for Tests C and D. Use this total and the chart below to determine your overall level in Mathematics. The chart also shows you how your level compares with the target level for your age group.

Total for Tests C and D

Level 4 or below	Level 5	Level 6	Level 7 or above
up to 30	31–49	50–84	85+
Working towards target level	Working at target level for age group		Working beyond target level

Marking Grid

TEST A — *Pages 2–16*

Question	Marks available	Marks scored	Question	Marks available	Marks scored
1	2		10	2	
2	6		11	2	
3	2		12	4	
4	1		13	3	
5	4		14	4	
6	2		15	6	
7	4		16	5	
8	3		17	5	
9	2		18	3	
			Total	60	

TEST B — *Pages 17–27*

Question	Marks available	Marks scored	Question	Marks available	Marks scored
1	4		11	3	
2	4		12	2	
3	2		13	4	
4	3		14	4	
5	2		15	2	
6	3		16	4	
7	2		17	2	
8	5		18	2	
9	2		19	6	
10	4		Total	60	

TEST C — *Pages 28–38*

Question	Marks available	Marks scored	Question	Marks available	Marks scored
1	6		8	5	
2	2		9	3	
3	4		10	4	
4	6		11	4	
5	2		12	6	
6	3		13	5	
7	6		14	4	
			Total	60	

TEST D — *Pages 39–50*

Question	Marks available	Marks scored	Question	Marks available	Marks scored
1	6		8	6	
2	3		9	3	
3	2		10	6	
4	6		11	3	
5	6		12	5	
6	1		13	4	
7	3		14	6	
			Total	60	